In at the Deep End

Published by Accent Press Ltd – 2009

ISBN 9781906373764

The Quick Reads project in Wales is a joint venture between Basic
Skills Cymru and the Welsh Books Council. Titles are funded through
Basic Skills Cymru as part of the National Basic Skills Strategy for
Wales on behalf of the Welsh Assembly Government.

Printed and bound in the UK

Cover design by Red Dot Design

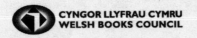

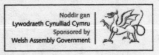

In at the Deep End:

From Barry to Beijing

David Davies

ACCENT PRESS LTD

Foreword

"David Davies. Remember the name."

These words, spoken by BBC Radio and Television presenter John Inverdale, have stuck in my mind ever since he made the comment at the Commonwealth Games in 2002. That was the occasion when a lanky seventeen-year-old Welshman caught the eye; you could sense there was something special about the young lad from Barry.

You will have to go a long way to find a more dedicated sportsman than David. As you will learn from this book, he doesn't compromise with his swimming, and he's had to make some hard choices along the way.

He has become Britain's most high-profile male swimmer of the twenty-first century, and quite rightly so. David is a true professional who knows his own mind; I feel privileged to have spent so much time in his company and to have covered his triumphs for BBC Radio.

This is not the end of his story, not by a long way!

Bob Ballard

Chapter One

A silver medal in Beijing

My first reaction was relief at getting to the end of the race. It was the hardest race I'd ever been in. Getting to the line was the only thing on my mind. When I touched the wall and realised I'd won an Olympic silver medal, well, it's a feeling you can't put into words.

I saw the winner, Maarten van der Weijden, hanging off the pole where you rest at the end of the race. I grabbed him, mostly just to stay afloat, but also to give him a hug. Then I hauled myself onto the pontoon so I could lie down, and I don't remember much else as I blanked out for a bit, feeling as though I wanted to be sick. It was not a nice feeling. I was dehydrated, low on sugar, exhausted, feeling hot; the lake temperature was 27 degrees centigrade. I was forced onto a stretcher, even though I wanted to be left there for a bit, and was then carried to the ambulance amid dramatic scenes.

3

My coach, Kevin Renshaw, was very emotional. He came to the ambulance and had a few tears in his eyes, bless him. He didn't have to say anything. We gave each other a hug and he said, "You've given it everything, you did yourself proud, you did me proud and have done everyone proud. Well done!"

I felt better when I came round and managed to enjoy the occasion, although I felt a bit rough for the rest of the day.

I was elated, really, as the 10k Open Water was a new race for me. There was massive joy and excitement and a lot of relief that those four years of work had not gone to waste. Having let things sink in, looking back at the race, I can see that an opportunity to win gold was there, but mistakes happened at the end. In the future, I can improve upon my performance. I've learned a lot. But at the time I definitely swam the race as hard as I could, and I gave everything, and that's what I am proud of. Standing on the Olympic podium was the happiest moment of my life; I've now been lucky enough to have done it twice.

Conditions for the men's race were very different from those for the women's race on the previous day. I spoke to the girls after my race and said I would rather have swum on their day because the weather was nice and sunny, a lot clearer, and I like swimming in the sunshine. They said, though, that the sun gets very annoying when it's really hot. However, I definitely found that the poor visibility in my race was a problem. But that's the beauty of Open Water swimming – you never know what conditions you're going to get.

I hadn't decided to do the event until January 2008, which is late to take up an event for the Olympics, in terms of preparation and planning for it. I'd been purely a pool-based swimmer all my career, so dealing with the changeable conditions of Open Water was going to be my biggest challenge. My coach Kevin and I came to the conclusion that the best way for me to do it was to swim from the front in water as clear as possible. If you're in front you're not getting bashed about by the other swimmers, not having to swim in a current nor getting someone's feet in your mouth. You're dictating the pace and where in the water you swim.

But it's also the hardest way to do it because you can't feed off everyone else, and you're doing all the work. I wanted to get into a rhythm for about eight kilometres and then build up speed over the last two and hope to split the pack.

The first seven and a half kilometres proved to be harder than I anticipated because the other swimmers were making it as tough as they could for me, moving up around me and making me swim faster than I actually wanted to if I was to stay in that clear water.

The best way to describe my physical state through that last thousand metres is a bit delirious and dizzy, not really knowing where I was going. I remember coming round the last turning buoy and thinking, right, this is the home straight, this is where I make my break. I put a big kick in, upped my stroke rate and immediately the pack reduced to just three or four swimmers. I knew then that I was in the medal hunt. But it took a lot out of me. I remember hitting the little rowing buoy markers which are about a metre apart. In trying to weave around them I nearly swam into the boat, and then I went back too far to the right, over-correcting myself. I was almost staggering my way to the line. I got through it when I finally saw the line, saw the funnel leading to it, and saw that at last the finishing pads were there. I thought: kick for home. I put in a second surge but by that time Maarten van der Weijden had passed me, swimming a perfect line, to finish ahead of me even though I was catching him during the last ten metres.

In 2007 I'd been adamant I didn't want to do the event. All my focus had been on the 1500 metres freestyle, which is the event for which I won an Olympic medal in Athens, and I didn't want anything to distract me from that. I thought the Open Water would be too difficult for me and it would affect my 1500.

However, I was persuaded, somehow, and the first race I tried, which was in South Africa, went well; I really enjoyed it and felt that I had more to give to Open Water swimming.

I did it again in the World Championships in Seville in May and came second, which qualified me for the Olympics. Then we more or less forgot about it because all my concentration was on the 1500.

I've said to Kevin, who'd been persuaded by Open Water Head Coach Sean Kelly that I should compete in the event, that their efforts to get me to swim the 10k could be the coaching decision they will remember for all time. It won me an Olympic medal and gave me an extra career path which will give me the chance to do bigger and better things over the next four years.

The reaction of many members of the public is that they can't believe that you can race around a lake for nearly two hours, when it's so physically demanding. People at home who stayed up in the middle of the night to watch have kindly described my swim as heroic, which is very flattering for me and, of course, good for interest in the sport. It can only grow with the event being staged in the Serpentine at the London Olympics.

The day we returned to Wales we had a ceremony down at Cardiff Bay, outside the Welsh Assembly where, on a work and school day, thousands of people turned out to greet us. They played a video of my race to the accompaniment of the song from the *Last Choir Standing* show, 'We Are the Champions', and it gave me goose bumps; it was surreal to be on an open-top bus and recognised on the street, but so exciting as well.

Looking back on it all, did I give myself too much to do, in swimming two tough 1500 metres races and then the Open Water? But it had never been done before, which was the kind of challenge that really attracted me. The event was new to the Olympics and there weren't many swimmers who would do both, and those that did were not expected to make the final in the pool – I was the only one who did.

They were two of the hardest 1500 metres races of my life. The heats were phenomenally fast. The time I recorded in my heat was only just slower than the time with which I won bronze in Athens and I only had thirty-six hours to recover and go again.

After starting well in the final, I faded to finish in sixth place. It had taken a lot out of me, not just physically, but emotionally too and then I had four days to get it right in the lake. I think the lake is where I showed my true character.

Chapter Two

My start in swimming

I was born in St David's Hospital, Cardiff, on 3rd March 1985, two days after St David's Day, hence my name. The first-born of my parents Paul and Sue, I have a younger sister, Sian.

My dad works in a silicone plant for Dow Corning as a pipe-fitter, and Mum works for South East Cancer Network. My little sister, who is five years younger than me, has started university in Cardiff.

Both my parents went to school in Barry and have lived there all of their lives. I went to a Welsh-language primary school before moving to an English-language secondary.

I'm very family orientated. I would visit my grandparents at weekends and they'd take me down to the beach on Barry Island on a Sunday morning and to the fairground. When I was seven my granddad took me down to Porthkerry Park, which is an enormous park in Barry, and I fell out of a tree and broke my arm.

I still have a huge scar on my arm from that operation.

I had a very normal childhood, really, and I was a very good boy, I'd like to say. I stayed out of trouble, had good friends and wasn't a problem child when it came to bullying or being loud in class – I was an 'average Joe'. Never top of the class but not bottom either.

I didn't enjoy going to school but, looking back now, it was a very good time. I enjoyed it more when I went to the English secondary school; it was quite weird learning things in Welsh.

But I must mention my A-level Welsh teacher, Mr Reynolds, who was a bit of character. I was the only pupil in the A-level class so I got to know him quite well. When he was reading your work he would start flicking your ear if he found a mistake and start tugging and twisting it. He'd say, "What are you doing, Dai squared?" – a joke reference to Dai, Dai for David Davies. He was an old Welsh traditionalist so if we were ever doing any Welsh poetry he'd start crying and get really emotional.

My P.E. teachers used to tell me I was a rugby boy and I should play on the wing. I'd say, "I'm not playing rugby, I can't injure myself, I'm a swimmer." They'd say, "You're not going to make it as a swimmer, get in there, get the ball, son, and run."

I used to play for the school second fifteen, standing out on the wing and trying not to get my hair wet or break a nail! (Bit of a diva.) But I did it just to be involved and keep the school happy.

Gradually they started saying, "You can sit out this rugby lesson, you're not a bad swimmer." John Huw Williams, my first P.E. teacher, and Rob Glaves, who was my P.E. teacher later on, were really keen and very supportive. Suddenly people stopped thinking, who is this joker who thinks he's a swimmer? And seemed to know everything about my rivals, and all of my achievements.

My school will claim that I was a gold-star pupil but I was really just run of the mill and I just got by. I wasn't into hanging around street corners and chucking stones at cars or drinking cider when thirteen. My childhood was all very quiet and enjoyable.

My first experience of swimming was when I was very, very young and we went to Portugal. Dad bought a fly-away football, threw it into the pool, then threw me in and told me to get

12

it. I didn't have any fear of the water and would swim on Dad's shoulders.

Mum got me involved in swimming at the local club in Barry. She was the swimmer of the family, having swum in her youth at District Schools' level, as well as for fun. I did the 'Learn to Swim' lessons and then went on to the Saturday galas when I was six or seven and I just loved the competing part of it.

I got into a winning habit quite early, it gave me a real thrill and I still have all my medals at home – Mum keeps them in a shoe box in the attic.

At school we did the Kellogg's badge awards when I was ten and by that time I was swimming at club level, so it was my chance to show off to the other kids in the class that I could swim. I got my gold badge at the 1500 metres, which was the longest distance you could swim.

The support parents give to their sporting kids is massively undervalued. It's not just about being taxi drivers, putting dinner on the table or buying a new pair of flash trainers at the weekend. My parents always gave me the right amount of support while being relaxed enough never to be pushy parents. They had enough knowledge of the sport to be able to advise me, without trying to tell me what to do. They would take me to swimming lessons and stay and watch while chatting to other parents. They'd come to watch at galas but whenever I got home I'd just be Dave as normal, whether I'd won or lost. They were definitely never pushy parents.

My parents have been huge influences on me. Their biggest influence, swimming-wise, was probably when they suggested I move from my local club in Barry and look to go somewhere else if I wanted to improve. This was indeed the start of a wonderful, much more serious swimming career.

Chapter Three

Competing as a junior

I left Barry and joined the City of Cardiff club at the age of nine, which for swimming in those days was like joining Real Madrid from Dagenham and Redbridge – for Welsh swimming, anyway.

Things were instantly different. Waking up early in the morning was the first thing I had to get used to. To this day I still find 5 a.m. starts hard work. The sound of an alarm buzzing when it's dark, wet and cold outside and you're in a deep sleep would make most kids switch off the alarm and go back to sleep. I got into a good habit early, however. I would get up, train, trot off to school, then return to the pool when school was over for the day.

I was finding the training work more enjoyable, more structured and could see myself swimming faster. There were a lot of talented kids at the club who were my age, so that gave me some competition and also gave me some very good friends. My oldest and best friends today are guys I met in my early days at Cardiff.

As a young kid I used to swim really high in the water with a short, fast, turn-over and I joined the Cardiff club in the lower ranks of swimmers. Of course, back then I had no vision of being in the Olympic Games. I was just there in order to improve my swimming; to be with better coaches at a better club.

But the Head Coach, Dave Haller, came in during one session, after I'd only just joined, and I remember him speaking to my mum and dad and the other coach and saying, "Don't change that boy's stroke. I know it's very unorthodox, but just leave him." That was a crucial moment in my career. After that Dave took an interest in me and always kept a close eye on me, and it gave me great confidence. He had only recently been on television, because he was our Head Coach at the World Championships in Rome in 1994, and a week later here he was, speaking to me. No wonder I was excited. So he's been an absolutely massive influence on me, right from the start. He is a visionary who has a fantastic eye for spotting technique and talent.

The best way to describe my stroke is that I swam like a spider crawls: really short strokes but with a very fast stroke rate.

It was natural for me and I have adapted it over the years. People used to say I wouldn't be able to keep that up, and no one could swim 200 and 400 freestyle like that, and I was just going to blow up. They thought that as soon as I put weight on I'd be lower in the water and wouldn't be able to do it.

I don't know if it was jealousy, or lack of understanding, but, in any case, I never really let it bother me.

We lived twenty minutes drive from the pool. I appreciated my parents' commitment driving me there twice a day, with early morning starts, and I know it put a strain on them.

Maybe knowing that pushed me on too. Because between the ages of nine and twelve I did very well at Welsh Age Group level. The big event of the year was always held at the Empire Pool and that was the event I particularly wanted to do well in. I got seven medals one year, eight the next and thought I was the bee's knees: this was as good as it got!

But when I was twelve I went for the first time to the British National Age Groups and suddenly went from being the big fish in a small pond to thinking that I'd never be as good as these kids. Several of them were very big at a young age and were absolutely miles ahead of me. I wasn't even making finals. I was finishing twelfth or thirteenth and I thought I was never going to make it.

But I kept going and when I was fifteen I made my first finals at National Age Groups and got two silver and two bronze medals. I thought this was brilliant. I framed the medals and thought that this would be as good as it got.

That was in 2000 and later that year I stayed up late to watch all the swimming at the Sydney Olympics and saw the Australian superstar Ian Thorpe, who was only a couple of years older than me. He swam a time of three minutes forty seconds for the 400 metres freestyle and I thought: that's ridiculously fast. It was so disheartening. It really hurt me. You're doing all those hours of swimming and then you see someone do something completely out of your league and you think, how does he do it, and how am I going to do it?

However, in the end it must have spurred me on, because I matured very quickly and knew I had to push on with my swimming career.

At sixteen I won my first National Age Group titles, in the 100, 200 and 400 metres freestyle and also the 400 metres individual medley. In addition I picked up two silver medals at the European Youth Olympics.

It was after having my first taste of international competition that I really knew that this was for me. I became much more dedicated in terms of the amount of training I was doing.

So, finally, everything clicked into place in 2002, when I was seventeen. I knew where I was going and I saw the path ahead of me.

Chapter Four

My first major Games

For the first time I was training ten times a week for two hours a session, and felt exhausted when I got home. But I had the satisfaction of having had a good work-out. And I was going into my races feeling very confident and I was knocking chunks and chunks of time off my personal bests that year. At the Commonwealth Games Trials in Manchester in April 2002, my personal best for the 400 metres freestyle was four minutes four seconds. In the heats I went three minutes fifty-five and was up against the big guns, Jamie Salter and Adam Faulkner. I was just behind them and finished fifth in the final.

That was one hell of a swim for me. I felt great because I'd qualified for the Commonwealth Games and also for the European Junior Championships in Linz, Austria, which were really important.

I won silver in the 400 metres freestyle and

a bronze in the 4 × 200 metres freestyle relay in Austria, again improving my times in both events.

Winning medals brings enormous confidence; if you're doing it at that level you feel you can go on to do it internationally.

Then I went to the Commonwealth Games in Manchester. They were all about enjoyment for me, getting experience and soaking up the fantastic home support we had. Although we were Welsh competitors coming into England, the home nations were all supportive of each other.

I did the 400 metres freestyle and I really wanted to make the final to experience the atmosphere. I finished tenth and swam slightly slower than I had at the European Juniors. I was a bit disappointed. I don't know whether nerves got to me or if I didn't warm up properly, but this was the first major event I'd been to, so perhaps I was expecting too much.

I had the 200 metre freestyle heats the next day, finishing ninth overall, but I swam much better. I felt I was improving as the Games went along, but, for me, with my races swum, it was now suddenly all over.

Then my coach Dave Haller said, "How do you fancy doing the 1500?" I saw the start list and there were only nine swimmers, one of whom was from Nigeria with a personal best of seventeen and a half minutes. I knew I could swim much faster and was almost guaranteed a place in the final. What else was I going to do for four days? I had an entry time for the event because I'd done a training swim earlier in the year. My personal best was fifteen minutes fifty-five seconds from that training swim and my plan was to cruise the heat, maybe come fourth or fifth, so that I could get a decent lane for the final. I went fifteen minutes thirty-three seconds, and it felt really, really easy. That time would have won a medal at the European Juniors a couple of weeks before, which made me think! I told Dave I felt really, really good and he said I'd swum very well, I'd looked great, looked natural in that event and we'd have a good laugh in the final the next day.

So I swam down, had a massage and got back to the Games village feeling really excited about what I'd done.

When it came to the final, I didn't feel out of place standing next to the top Australian Grant Hackett or Britain's 1996 Olympic silver medallist, Graeme Smith. I loved walking out to the noise of the crowd, with my name being announced. That gave me goose bumps.

It's the race I'll remember for the rest of my life as my first big one. I swam fifteen minutes seventeen seconds, another eighteen seconds off my best – which meant I'd taken nearly forty seconds off in two days! I came sixth, breaking the Welsh record, and it made me believe that, although I wasn't close to Hackett then, in time, I could be.

All the applause was going to Hackett for winning the Commonwealth title, but I felt like some of it was for me for doing so well. I couldn't see any Welsh flags in the crowd but as I got out of the pool I saw the Wales team in the far corner going absolutely mad. All the Australian coaches went up to Dave and said it was a great swim and the National Performance Director, Bill Sweetenham, whom I'd never really spoken to before, said the same and I was flattered.

Things kept getting better after that. I went to the British Short Course Championships in Cambridge just a couple of weeks later and in the 1500 metres beat a man I'd admired and who was my role model, Graeme Smith.

I was in the lane next to him and managed under fifteen minutes. The crowd stood up, I got interviewed on poolside – it was all new to me, the whole media thing. That's when I had to make the transition from being a talented junior to being part of the senior team.

I made the European Short Course team for Riesa, Germany, in December 2002. I didn't want to go there just to make up the numbers and loved the atmosphere, the spotlight, the crowd and the noise, and being part of a big event. I took another twelve seconds off my personal best in the 1500 metres freestyle, clocking fourteen minutes forty-two seconds and coming second to the Russian, Yuri Prilukov, a big rival of mine.

The best thing about that meeting was that I was voted 'Best Newcomer' by the European swimming media, and received an award.

I was on cloud nine and when I returned home I was buzzing from the whole experience. Now I wanted more and more.

Chapter Five

International success

After Riesa, the target was the British Championships again, which also doubled up as trials for the World Championships. The qualifying standards were pretty stiff and it was going to be the first meeting where I actually had a proper senior swimmers' 'taper'. (A 'taper' is a slow-down in training. I'll explain properly what it is later in the book.)

I knew I would be racing Graeme Smith again. We'd become big rivals very quickly because of my rapid ascent. We had three absolutely epic races in the 400 metres freestyle along with Adam Faulkner. We all swam very close to each other in the 400 metres and I took three seconds off my best there, finishing in three minutes fifty-one seconds. Graeme won it in three minutes forty-nine and Adam was second in three minutes fifty.

In the 1500 metres I dropped twelve seconds to clock fifteen minutes five seconds and Graeme just beat me by a few tenths of a second. It was a really close race; we were neck and neck the whole way. Sometimes he would edge ahead and then I would edge ahead. He tried to break me and I would try and do the same to him but his experience and that bit more strength at the end meant that he just beat me to the touch.

I didn't really know him that well at that time, but he came across and gave me a big hug at the end. Graeme knew that it was a very special swim for me and he was happy because he had shown some form, which he hadn't done at the end of 2002. We were good for each other. He was at the back end of his career and I was starting mine, so it was perfect timing.

And, most importantly, I'd qualified for the World Championships. I had always expected to, but the job was done and now I could get on with it.

We also raced the 800 metres freestyle that year, which was live on BBC Television. Graeme just beat me again and the race was very similar to the 1500. I remember Sharron Davies, a silver medallist from the 1980 Olympics in Moscow, who was doing the interviews, saying: "Well, there's the old Scottish braveheart just touching out the

Welsh pretender, but I don't think he'll be pretending for much longer – he's a real star to look out for."

That remark made all the people who watched it back home, and my friends who don't normally watch swimming say things like, "Actually, Dave, you're not bad at swimming, are you?" They had been winding me up for years, saying things like, "You just put a pair of trunks on and run around poolside playing games". But I'd proved that I worked hard, and they started to understand and respect what I did.

However, I was still only eighteen and also had A levels to do at school. I came away with an 'A' and two 'B's in History, Welsh as a second language, and Physical Education. I also managed to achieve a sixty per cent attendance record even though I was away a lot swimming and trained so much. Credit must go to my parents for helping me fit it all in and to Dave Haller, who was steering me and directing me and keeping my feet on the floor. He encouraged me to take each day as it came, not allowing me to get too stressed.

In July 2003 Barcelona staged the World Swimming Championships.

This was a step up from the Commonwealth Games because now the whole world was competing, including a really big team from the United States of America, along with established names from Europe. The event took place over eight days, also something I'd never experienced before. I had to learn to keep my focus till the last day, while going through the shared emotions of the team, supporting them, and sitting through the long sessions.

I had been a pretty popular guy on the junior team, but now I was with people much older than me in a seasoned international team. I was the youngest of the boys there by a fair bit, so it was hard to fit in. You see people like the experienced butterfly swimmer Steve Parry and you know he's funny because you've seen him on the television and you feel you know him, but of course you don't. But he was great at bringing me into the conversation and I built up a great bond with him.

I roomed with the Scottish swimmer Gregor Tait, who was six years older than me. That was a test as he was in a swim-off for a place in the final of the 200 metres backstroke and he lost the race. He came back, couldn't sleep, and was up all night. I was thinking, what do I do, I'm swimming tomorrow, shall I speak to him? But, in the end, we were fine. We often talk about that now as we are quite good friends and even lived together for a while when he moved to Cardiff.

I made the final of the 1500 metres freestyle, though I didn't think I was going to. I went a bit slower in the heat – I thought I could ease up, which I shouldn't have done, and got touched out in my heat. In the final I swam slightly better than my personal best, but, because of the way I'd been swimming, with big decreases in my times, I'd expected another big drop. I came fourth, which was good going for a first World Championships, but I felt I had too much energy left at the end. I'm not sure if that was down to the way I swam the race, but I had definitely expected more.

However, I didn't dwell on it as I had the European Junior Championships straight afterwards in Glasgow, and flew there from Barcelona.

I was made the Great Britain team captain. It was a nice honour to be chosen by my peers. You have to be seen as a decent guy, approachable and likeable, and I did all I could to get good team chemistry. It's all about enjoyment. You won't swim fast unless you're happy.

I was going for the same record that 1996 Olympic bronze medallist Paul Palmer achieved when he was my age. He won the 200, 400 and 1500 metres freestyle and they were the events I was doing.

I came second in the 200 and swam very well, achieving a personal best time. I was third in the 400 even though I swam an absolute shocker of a race, three seconds off my best time. I don't know what happened to me; the winner came from lane eight and second place was in lane one, whereas I was in the lane for the fastest swimmer, lane four.

Then came the main event, the 1500. I led out from the front and went on to win the race. I'd won the European Juniors! It was a massive relief, because for the first time I felt I was the favourite for a race, which hadn't happened before.

I'd done it in front of a home crowd; my mum and dad were there and some family from Scotland had come along as well. It was brilliant. I loved the national anthem being played, the standing ovation and the lap of honour afterwards.

I remember we had a team meeting and

somebody said that European Junior champions generally go on to great things. They had a list of the names that had been successful: Paul Palmer, Graeme Smith and Steve Parry from Britain, all of them top internationals. It made me think that I was on the right track.

Chapter Six

Disappointments

There is a big difference between being part of a junior team and being in the seniors.

As a junior you're almost spoon-fed in terms of your pool training – you're taken through every step.

When you're a senior you have to be a lot more independent, and you have to manage yourself a lot more. You can't afford to stop and stare because it's so fast and furious. You have to be at breakfast on time, make sure everything is packed in your bag because you might not come straight back from the pool. There are media commitments, doping tests, everything to do. You can do all the preparation you like, but until you experience it you can't really know what to expect.

Having made big improvements in times to get to this kind of level, some athletes now reach their plateau period. Also your body is going through big changes in your late teens.

One day you can do your training and feel fine, and another day you can be tired and sore and feel unable to do the work.

It was frustrating as I didn't understand why I couldn't swim well every session. One day I could do fifty-eight seconds for one hundred metres and be flying, and the next week it would be sixty, or sixty-one, seconds.

I'm not the type to totally lose my cool, but I was very frustrated, especially coming up to the World Championships. I wanted to be swimming fast and kept wondering what I was doing wrong.

I probably sulked, to be honest. Swimming dictates my mood so much. I wish it didn't, but I can't help it, it just does. If I swim a fantastic session, on the drive home I'll sing along to every song on the radio, whereas if I have had a nightmare of a set I'll be hunching my shoulders and acting like Kevin the teenager from the Harry Enfield show!

I try to keep it to myself, just muttering stuff under my breath. I don't take it out on anyone else. If I'd swum well I would come in and tell my mum, but if I hadn't I'd just be quiet and in a mood. She soon worked out what it was all about.

After the break following the World Championships, we had a training camp in Australia and I swam absolutely terribly. I was training with Graeme Smith and he was beating me in every session.

I got ill from trying too hard.

It was meant to be an early-season camp for me to get fit, but I was thinking about the Olympics the following year and that I had to train hard, and I was getting really wrapped up in it.

I had a bad period leading up to December. In the 1500 metres at the European Short Course Championships in Dublin, an event where I'd come second a year earlier, I swam twenty seconds slower, got lapped by the winner, got beaten by Graeme Smith, came eleventh overall and felt absolutely terrible in the water.

I saw my mum and dad and cried, which I don't normally do. I thought, I've had my run, it's all over; I didn't know what was happening.

Dave Haller gave me a few days off to let things sink in and have a rest. We came to the conclusion that I'd over-trained, tried too hard, too early and needed to chill out and start enjoying myself. I needed to remember what I'd done the previous year, and just let it happen.

I had a very low-key Christmas, just plodding along and enjoying my time with the family. When I went back to the pool in January a sports scientist, Bob Treffene, came over for three weeks from Australia to work with me. I'd met Bob previously but never worked with him.

He must be up there in terms of influence on my career, along with Dave, but for very different reasons. His experience working with Olympic champions from Australia, Kieren Perkins and Grant Hackett, made me instantly respect him, and when he talked he made sense. We had a bond straight away. Doing the training sessions he was giving me I could see the improvement immediately. And after he left I was swimming the kind of sets I expected to be swimming, very fast, and getting better each week.

In February 2004 I went to the American National Championships and raced a swimmer called Larsen Jensen whom I'd beaten in the 1500 metres freestyle the previous year, though he had swum a personal best in the 800. He was a good young swimmer, like I was, and taking him on in his home country was a big thing for me.

In the race he was miles ahead of me but he

'died' and I came back to finish first in fifteen minutes two seconds. So I'd gone from a massive disappointment at the European Short Course, three months earlier, to swimming really well.

Then we went down to Fort Lauderdale to have a training camp and I swam wonderfully for two weeks. I came back buzzing from both the earlier race, and from the training.

We were constantly in touch with Bob Treffene and the model of training that we'd set up was working, and working very well.

I got to the Olympic Trials in Sheffield in April expecting to qualify. It would have been a huge shock to me and, I'm sure, to others if I hadn't made it. But the question was, having swum so fast unrested, could I dip under fifteen minutes? Could I break Graeme Smith's British record of fourteen minutes fifty-eight seconds, or could I do something really special and go down to a time in the low fourteen fifties?

I thought I was capable of doing it at that time, although I was a bit over-rested. I'd missed out on the 400 metres freestyle but it was all about the 1500, nothing else mattered.

In the final I went out for it and knew I was going to win straight away, knew I was going to swim under fifteen minutes. I remember that with the last one hundred metres to go I was on thirteen minutes fifty-eight; the crowd went absolutely wild. Every coach, every swimmer, was waving. I remember breathing towards them every time for inspiration. The roar was enormous and when I finished the feeling was one of relief because it was all over. The Olympic trials are so emotional and it doesn't matter how confident you are, even if you know you're going to get it, it's still a massive relief when it's all done.

I gave Mum a hug, Dad a hug and Dave a hug because even he was emotional. Now we could move on again.

Chapter Seven

Heading for Athens

Before we move on to the lead-up to Athens and the Olympics in 2004, there's something I should explain. You will see the word 'taper' mentioned a few times in this book, and it's something swimmers often refer to ... so what is it?

A taper starts three weeks out from a big meeting, and it means that each week the training volume will come down. For example, from seventy-five thousand metres of swimming to sixty-five thousand the next week, then to fifty-five and between forty-five and fifty thousand metres in the final week.

Also the distance of my main sets, the individual parts of sessions, will come down from three thousand metres the first week to two and a half thousand and gradually decrease, with the balance of the swims changing from endurance-based to speed-based as you become more race-specific. You get a couple of lie-ins as well.

The reason we taper is that when we train, we train very hard and very intensively. Your body is not sharp, it's in training mode and not ready to race. To get it into race mode you have to step your training down so that your muscles become rested. When they are not feeling so tired, they get more speed and become more charged. So when you race you feel very fresh, very sharp and after you shave down and put your racing suit on you're in the best shape you can be.

I loved every minute of the Athens experience and took it all in my stride. It all made sense. Not just the two weeks of the Olympics, but the whole year before that. After qualifying I went straight away with the team on an Olympic preparation camp in France. Then I came back to Cardiff, had a long weekend off to celebrate with friends and family, and went back to work. There wasn't a day that went by without the motivation of the Olympics on my mind. You just couldn't escape from it.

Letters arrived telling us what was happening, what to expect, the itinerary, when to pick up the team kit.

My dad drove me up to Earls Court in London in my little Corsa to pick up that kit.

I expected a few T-shirts and a suitcase to go to the Olympics with. We actually came back with a great big suitcase in the passenger seat; I was crammed into the rear with boxes, other bags, and all the other kit.

In all, we had 50–60 kg of kit, which included everything you could possibly imagine. Although we were going to Athens, we had fleeces, hoodies, coats and gloves! It was amazing. And it was all really good stuff. I remember unpacking it and my dad saying, "Can I have one those T-shirts?" Then my sister saying, "I'll have that polo shirt," and the next day my gran coming down and claiming, "I can play golf in that." "Let me wear it first," I said. "When I come back from Athens I'll see what I can do for you."

I trained really well for the three weeks at the Olympic training camp in Cyprus. I think that's where I won my Olympic medal. I met up again with Bob Treffene and the training was both consistent and consistently good. I was able to compare notes with Bob as he had Kieren Perkins's training records and I was actually on a par, if not slightly better than he was. That gave me enormous confidence. Also

I loved training with Graeme Smith in a fifty-metre outdoor pool in the sun. All I had to do was to be patient.

We went to Cyprus again just before going into Athens. It was a week earlier than everyone else. It was quiet, very low-key, just getting on with the business, swimming on my own, very relaxed, being looked after by Dave and Bob, my two grumpy pensioners. We all knew I was going to swim well, with just a bit of fine-tuning needed here and there.

When I finally got to Athens I went up to the Olympic village with the rest of the team. Dave and Bob were staying in a hotel as they didn't have accreditation. The plan was that every day I would meet them at an off-site pool and do my training and just go on my own to the competition pool.

This worked so well – there was a lot of drama in the British swimming team around the pool as some things had not gone well. Some of the coaches were upset and there was conflict with the National Performance Director, Bill Sweetenham, who was a fiery character. But fortunately I was out of all the drama.

Chapter Eight

A great day

When it came to race day I was totally ready.

I didn't know about expectations resting on me as I wasn't aware of what the media was saying. I wasn't reading the papers or watching television, not answering my phone or reading texts.

Race day was all about what I wanted to do. I wasn't thinking about medals too much. I knew there were four guys who could win medals and I was one of the four. I was on the start list but you never know what is going to happen.

The guys around me when I went to watch other finals were saying things like, "He's our only hope now", "It's Luke Skywalker", "Don't leave him alone; don't let him hurt his leg or anything." But it was only wind-up banter and I didn't think too much about it.

Steve Parry had won our only medal, a

bronze in the 200 metres butterfly, but there had been a lot of other disappointments, and the team had got really down.

The heats were on a Friday morning on a boiling hot day. Again I was down at the pool on my own; I warmed up by myself, with Dave in the stand. He said, "Morning, son, are you alright?" and I was totally relaxed. It's funny looking back at it now, but we were just ready to go.

I felt great in warm-up, got my swimsuit on and went down to the 'call room'. It didn't bother me at all. I saw my main opponents, Larsen Jensen, Grant Hackett, Yuri Prilukov, all of the big guns in the race, and then walked out onto the pool deck. I felt comfortable in the arena.

I was in lane four for the first heat, and was about half a body-length up by fifty metres, a body-length up by one hundred and felt in a very good rhythm swimming the fastest heat time ever, a British record of fourteen minutes fifty-seven seconds.

When I finished I felt that it had been unbelievably easy, an absolute doddle. I was cruising most of the race. I got out of the pool with a lot of energy and had to calm myself down. I did a quick interview and got through the media area, which is called the mixed zone. Dave Haller said to me, "That was easy, wasn't it? Just making sure, because it did look really easy."

I said, "It was, I promise you it was easy." Dave told me to go and swim down; he and Bob were starting to get excited now. They were trying to climb over the barriers with anxiety, wanting to get me away from the press and distractions from the job in hand.

Somebody informed me how the other heats were going – that my time would have won the second heat, and when the last heat came in they didn't swim under fifteen minutes either. I was the fastest qualifier and knew I'd be in lane four for the final.

I still couldn't see anyone outside the main four swimmers getting a medal and I knew that I was in great form. I knew I would go a lot quicker in the final, which was taking place in the evening of the next day.

The day of the final was a lonely one. Most of the swimmers had finished their events and I had to stay away from them and I didn't have my coach in the Village. I went down to breakfast on my own, and then for a light paddle at the pool. There wasn't much said between Dave and me, just a couple of reminders about technique, turns, and not being out of the race at the start.

In the afternoon I went down to the pool early on my own. It was bizarrely quiet because there were only a couple of events left, so I had a lane to myself to warm up in.

It all clicked into place for the final. It was one of my best performances to date and I won the bronze medal. If I'd gone out a bit more quickly maybe I could have won gold. That's with hindsight, but I don't believe I gave it my all in that race.

I felt almost embarrassed to be on the feet and then the hips of Grant Hackett, having been five metres back at one stage. Larsen Jensen and I churned it out between us. Maybe I should have gone with him and then had a go at Hackett.

I touched the wall and I knew I'd got my medal. In fact I knew I had one with two hundred and fifty metres to go, once Yuri Prilukov had been dropped.

When I finished I looked round and it was like the scoreboard was spinning. I didn't know what to do. I don't show emotion very well, but my instant reaction was to say well done to Hackett. I jumped on him and banged him on the head like he was a dog or something. Then all of a sudden I was hugging Larsen; I was all over the place.

Graeme Smith, who had been in lane one, came over to me and I didn't know what to say. I was hugging him and looking around thinking I might spot Mum and Dad in the crowd although I didn't have a clue where they were.

On the medal podium I saw Dave and Bob in the crowd and waved to them, got the accolades from the GB team, and threw them the flowers that are presented to the medal winners. I was on a total high that night. I went to the BBC studio to do an interview and afterwards didn't get to bed.

The next day it started to sink in. I read all the messages on my phone, eighty-four of them. I didn't realise I knew that many people! That's when you feel you've done something special – for them as well as for yourself.

I watched the race so many times when I got home, and the more times I watched it, the more what I'd achieved sank in.

Chapter Nine

World Championships

I had a very short break after the Olympics. I had pretty strong motivation to get back into the pool. Winning the medal hadn't turned my head too much and I got back into fitness really quickly.

I found some early form at the European Short Course Championships in Vienna, breaking the British record, clocking fourteen minutes thirty-two seconds, which was the fifth fastest time ever then.

I thought, I'm on the right track, being ahead of where I was at the same time the previous year, and it looked like being a good year.

In early 2005, when the World Championship trials were being held, I again suffered the problem that I'd had before, from trying too hard. When I was tapering I was forcing myself and arrived in Manchester not feeling very fresh, and consequently not swimming very well.

By now Graeme Smith had retired and I was a good minute ahead of the rest of the field in the UK. That was now something I had to deal with. It was just me against the clock – it's not the best drive going into a race knowing that you're going to win comfortably. You want to be challenged and extended, although I didn't want to be arrogant about it. But that's how it has remained in home races for a good few years.

Despite winning in Manchester by a big margin, in what was a very lonely race, I only managed to swim a time of fifteen minutes seven seconds, some twenty-two seconds off my best, which meant I only just scraped the qualifying time for the World Championships at Montreal, which was a pretty stiff time that year. I had to achieve a time that would have put me in the top ten in the world in 2004.

It was a horrendous swim, and I was annoyed and upset because I wanted to perform well in front of the home crowd. I wanted to show that I wasn't a one-off. But I did make it to the World Championships. Dave, Bob and I reviewed my race and we realised the errors that I'd made.

I had a very good summer after that, leading up to Montreal, which was all about underlining and repeating what I'd done before.

The same guys, minus Graeme, would be at the World Championships and I didn't want to be the one who'd dropped off from the Olympics. I wanted to be the swimmer who had moved on.

I was probably in as good a shape as I'd been in Athens. But I decided to swim the race a bit differently, going out a lot slower, giving Hackett, Prilukov and Jensen a good couple of body-lengths up to the halfway stage. I was clocking one minute for every one hundred metres whereas a year before I'd been recording times in the low fifty-nine second range.

I did, however, come back a lot more quickly, in seven minutes fifty seconds, a time that was faster than my swim in the 800 metres freestyle and better than the British record.

I'd clawed my way back into the medals after we dropped Prilukov. Hackett wasn't going to be caught this time – he had one of his best years that year. I was a few body-lengths behind Jensen but managed to pull level with the American and then pulled away from him into the last one hundred metres.

On the last turn it must have looked to most people as if the silver was mine for the taking, but I didn't have a sprint finish and, even though I had Jensen beaten, I couldn't finish him off.

He gave a big strong leg kick at the end and managed to touch me out for second place.

Did I swim that race the right way? I don't know. Once again I came home with far too much energy left. I still hadn't had my perfect race and had picked up the bronze medal again. Really I should have been a bit more disappointed and angry at myself for letting Jensen come back like that, but I was satisfied to have won bronze again and proved that the Olympics wasn't a one-off. I was third in the world against some really good swimmers.

Looking back on it now, I showed weakness. I didn't have a lot of speed. I was an endurance swimmer while these guys were bigger and had the ability to do good four hundreds and eight hundreds and had fast finishes over the last fifty metres.

For the team it could have been one of the low points in the relationship with the National Performance Director, Bill

Sweetenham. We were going through a big change with a lot of retirements after Athens and the selection policy made it very hard to get on the team, so it was a very small team – only about ten of us. There were a lot of new faces, Liam Tancock, Caitlin McClatchey and Kate Heywood, the first two of them winning bronze medals. But there were huge disappointments and again some internal bickering in the camp.

But I could laugh at it because I was never directly involved with it. Dave Haller kept me away from it all. We got on with our job and did it very well.

As a person I was now much more mature, and a lot more independent. I felt I'd grown up really quickly. I'd got the values I wanted and the professionalism and the drive to achieve my goals.

I felt that people had a new-found respect for me, having won the Olympic medal. In fact a lot of people were stunned by what I'd achieved. And of course I got more attention. More people wanted to talk to me, which was fine, although you have to work out who wants to talk to you for valid reasons, not just because you're an Olympic medallist.

Chapter Ten

Commonwealth gold, but at a price

Towards the end of 2005 Australian Swimming announced that Grant Hackett wouldn't be competing at the Commonwealth Games in Melbourne and I was genuinely disappointed because it's his home country, his home pool and I wanted to take him down while swimming for Wales. It would have been a fairy-tale story.

Once he had pulled out, I was favourite to win the 1500 metres freestyle, which, in itself, brings extra pressure. Also, if I won they would say that I only won the event because Hackett wasn't there. I was in a no-win situation.

But that was the way it was – there was nothing I could do about it. I still approached it as an important meeting because it was the midway point towards the next Olympics.

I did a lot more hard work, with my goal a crack at Kieren Perkins's Commonwealth

Games record which was fourteen minutes forty-one seconds, the second fastest time of all time. If I got that it would be another major breakthrough, moving me up among the big guns of distance swimming.

We went out to Australia very early and spent seven weeks on the Gold Coast in Brisbane before going to Melbourne to prepare. The whole time I felt under pressure which I didn't enjoy, but I couldn't get away from it. Even the locals were telling me that I was the Welsh guy who was going to win and at team meetings they would be saying, "When David wins." I would say, "Hang on – we haven't even got to Melbourne yet!"

I had a lot of phone interviews to do, not only with the British press but the Australian as well. There is a huge interest in distance swimming there and, with Hackett not competing, I was the favourite and they wanted to speak to me.

For the first time I saw Dave Haller feel the pressure. We really weren't enjoying it. We were there far too long and couldn't escape from it and by the time it was over we felt "Thank God that's done". It wasn't the joyous moment it should have been.

At the time I expected so much of myself. I

probably put more pressure on myself than anyone from the outside put on me. I wanted to prove something to someone who wasn't even there – Grant Hackett.

You can only beat who's up against you, which I did, but I wanted a lot more.

It was a good arena and a good atmosphere. It did have an international feel and it was a proud moment when I won but as I was swimming I knew my time wasn't going to be fast. I went under fifteen minutes, which was nice and respected by the crowd, but what I really wanted was to be able to say to Grant Hackett, who was in the stands, "What do you think of that?"

Representing Wales is different from swimming for Great Britain. It's like a vacation, or, put another way, Britain is my bread and butter but performing for Wales is only once every four years so the heart beats just as fast, but it's a different type of beat, a very patriotic one.

The Welsh national anthem is one of the most emotional anthems around. I found that it made my bottom lip tremble and I could feel the whole waterworks building up, I couldn't smile.

Afterwards my mum asked me why I hadn't

smiled, and I told her I was trying not to cry. But I did really enjoy it. There were so many Welsh flags being waved as I was doing my lap of honour, I couldn't believe it. One of the flags had 'Dai the fish' on it.

The Commonwealth Games has such an enjoyable, laid-back kind of atmosphere. Everybody knows each other, everybody speaks English and they really are a "friendly" Games. There is so much attention from Wales. Welsh people love their sport, they love their successful sportsmen and they give us tremendous coverage and support.

I had a few days off from swimming when I got back from Melbourne. I was walking around London when I realised that my foot was hurting badly. I wasn't sure if it was the shoes that I was wearing but when I took them off there was a big black lump on my ankle. My first reaction was that I must have banged it, so I put some ice on the foot expecting it to be better the next day. But instead it got worse.

I kept walking on it until the pain became unbearable. It was constantly throbbing and hurting me. One night I was up at one o'clock in the morning with my foot in an ice cold bath, reading a book because I couldn't sleep. My mum decided to take me hospital. By the minute the pain got more unbearable. I was nearly crying with it.

The hospital gave me strong painkillers and I had blood tests and they kept me in overnight. They also did an ultrasound scan on my ankle; that's what they use to test the health of unborn babies. They showed the scan on a screen and told me there was a lot of infection – muck, basically – gathered in a big abscess which would need surgery.

I was on an intravenous drip to calm the infection down but I still needed surgery, not once, but twice, because they had to open my foot up, clear all the muck out and then leave it open for the wound to seep.

Then, a couple of days later I had to go back in again to have the infection cleaned and the foot was only stitched halfway up so that the wound could seal from the inside out.

All this meant I had an open wound which would prevent me from swimming for seven weeks. It was unheard of; I'd never ever had seven weeks off, seven weeks out of the water!

Chapter Eleven

Fighting back

The real downside from the injury was that I wouldn't be able to go to the European Championships – I wouldn't be fit enough for the next big meeting.

I'd never been to the senior European Championships before and it was the only other championship I needed to complete my set of major international medals. It was hard to take, but we tried to put a positive spin on it. At least it hadn't happened in Olympic year and jeopardised my chances of another Olympic medal.

I hoped I would be able to take advantage of the break, recharge and come back better than ever. But the seven weeks off were so boring, so long. I had no direction in my life, sitting there with a cast on, watching daytime television. I couldn't even move around the house.

Naturally I put weight on, and as soon as I could I was doing some exercise in the gym, one-legged cycling, one-legged rowing. But it wasn't the same. I wasn't getting the same buzz from it. I used to go and watch the guys swim but that got me down even more. I couldn't even enjoy doing things with my mates as I was on crutches.

However, in all that time I never felt like quitting, although it would have been the easy option. I knew I had a lot more to give. I was only twenty-one; I would get over it. I just had to be persistent and patient.

After the seven weeks off, when I got back into the pool I felt absolutely terrible. It took so long to get the feel back, to get the weight off and to get the fitness back. It was also hard to watch the British team swim in Budapest. I was at home on my own as Dave Haller was with another swimmer, Gregor Tait, so I had to go to the pool on my own and train with no real motivation. It was a depressing time. In fact, it was horrible.

But, on the other hand, while the swimmers who had been at the European Championships were on their break, I was still swimming, and when they returned I was ahead of them.

Now I felt like I was back in the game. I went to Australia for seven weeks to do some good training with Bob Treffene and the British men's team. I got really fit and came back in December to prepare for what was to be my trial for the World Championships. Everybody else had qualified via their times at the European Championships, but I had a late exemption because of my injury and was allowed to do a qualifying swim in Eindhoven, Holland. I swam fourteen minutes fifty-five seconds, which was the quickest time I did that year and the fourth fastest in the world that year.

Given where I was and that I hadn't fully tapered for it, which meant there was still more to come from me, I was very encouraged and very happy and knew I was back.

So, having qualified, the next step for me was the World Championships in Melbourne which were to take place in April 2007. I hadn't really taken in during the Commonwealth Games what a great sporting city Melbourne is. It's sports-mad. There were posters everywhere advertising the swimming with pictures of the Australian superstars Grant Hackett and Leisel Jones, and other top swimmers, on billboards around the city.

You know it's big when you get a police escort from the airport to the hotel!

The event was being staged at the Rod Laver Arena, better known for hosting the Australian Open tennis championships. To have a pool in it seemed daft, how did they do that?

My first reaction was 'Wow'. It was a really good environment, a great setting and an electric atmosphere. To this day it's one of the best places I have ever swum.

I enjoyed it more than my previous trip to Melbourne. I was just pleased to be there, happy to be on the team. I didn't feel under much pressure, didn't feel I had much to prove.

Again my event was at the back end of the programme; I would swim at the weekend, when there was a full house for both the heats and the final.

The Australians consider the 1500 metres freestyle an event they own, so once again I would be up against the national hero in Grant Hackett. I knew he was off form, but that Yuri Prilukov had swum amazingly well in December, so I thought he was going to move the event on.

As for me, I hadn't competed much, only once since the Commonwealth Games, when I qualified in Eindhoven, so I expected to be a bit rusty.

I was relaxed about it all; I just wanted to enjoy it and see what I could do.

I watched the heats and saw that the best times were under fifteen minutes. I'd been the only person who had ever done that before. That raised the stakes and I knew that I would have to win my heat, which was the last of twelve. It was nearly one o'clock in the afternoon by the time I swam. I was like a little rabbit in a hutch just waiting to go.

When I got in I felt good. I worked hard, perhaps, with hindsight, just a little too hard, and finished in fourteen minutes fifty-three seconds, my third fastest time ever. I'd wrapped up the heat early but had kept going because I felt I had something to prove to myself – quite what, I don't know. That time meant I was fastest going into the final.

People were saying it was the best I'd looked in a long time and they were very excited about what I could do the next day. The Australian media thought I would win it. I thought that I had a massive chance. With Hackett not on top form, who else was in the frame? Larsen Jensen had looked really good in the heats, Prilukov just sneaked in in lane one, and then there was the Polish guy, Mateusz Sawrymowicz, who had shown some early season form. I thought that the race was pretty wide open. If I had something left in me, I could win.

National Performance Director Bill Sweetenham said, "It's yours for the taking. You look great, it's the best that I have ever seen you."

But the heat had taken more out of me than I had expected. Whether it was a fitness thing or that I forced myself too early, I don't know, but I didn't feel as fresh.

I did go quicker in the final, to finish third, a result I would have welcomed when I was lying in hospital, feeling down, the year before, but now I was left with the feeling I could have done better. The best thing about it was that I had pre-qualified for the Olympic Games; a top four place in Melbourne meant that you were automatically in the team for Beijing.

The drama of having to achieve the qualifying time at the Olympic trials was out of the way. I was definitely going and had eighteen months to prepare for it.

Chapter Twelve

A change of scene

My decision to move from Cardiff to Loughborough surprised a lot of people.

But I'd found that my life had become automatic, repetitive and routine. I was getting up, going training, swimming, coming home, eating food, going to bed, training again, going to bed again. I wasn't enjoying it and I didn't have the same drive as I used to have.

I thrive off a good atmosphere, good training sets and moving on but I'd grown out of the club environment. Suddenly the guys around me weren't my age any more. They were aged fourteen or fifteen and I was no longer a teenager; I was twenty-two. I felt I wanted to go out with a few friends, not to drink but to stay out later than I normally would. I wanted to have a laugh.

Training started to suffer because I was missing sessions, which was really unlike me. But I realised that something wasn't right.

While I was moping around the house my mother managed to get it all out of me. She said, "You know what you have to do."

I said, "I can't leave, that's unheard of." She told me that I would only get one shot at it; could I really see myself continuing this way for a year? She said, "Especially when you don't want to do it, is it going to work?"

My response was, "I'll do it, because it's the Olympics." Mum responded by telling me that it was easy to say that, but it would be tough and that I had to do what was right for me.

I talked to Dave, my coach, and he was very unhappy about what I had to say. It was one of the hardest conversations I've ever had in my life. I didn't want to hurt him but I had to be honest. I let him know that I was unhappy and he pointed to all the achievements I'd made over my long period in Cardiff. He told me he had been around the block a few times and knew what he was doing. But my restlessness was nothing to do with him. I totally respected him as a coach and what he had done for me and still, to this day, believe he is one of the best coaches we have in British swimming. For me the problem was the whole experience, my life, the environment I was in, the routine I was living. I needed something extra to make me kick on and try to improve on what I'd already done. It had been three years since I'd had a personal best time in my main event.

The prospect of a new fifty-metre pool in Cardiff didn't alter my thinking. After all, I'd trained in a twenty-five metre pool and achieved an Olympic bronze medal three years earlier.

In the end Dave was really good about me leaving. He said, "Move on then. Do what you need to do. Just make sure you train hard and do what you have to do for next year." He had some suggestions as to where I should go. I also consulted Bob Treffene, because he's a big part of my career and my life, and is also a good friend. We came to the conclusion that I should go up to Loughborough; it's where half of the British team swim.

But those last few sessions in Cardiff were hard for both of us.

Dave was working with swimmers who were going to the National Youth Championships and I was preparing for a meeting in Japan. As I was seeing out my time at the club I was left to my own devices.

There was so much we could have said. I told him how thankful I was for all he'd done for me, and he responded by saying, "You owe me nothing."

He had not only helped me as a swimmer but as a person growing up and was an enormous influence on my life. He used to take me to school sometimes; he got me my first sponsorship deal, took me down to his golf course a few times and was always looking out for me.

I also knew it was going to be hard to move away from my family. I'd always lived at home and had all my family around me but I didn't want to be around them when I was unhappy. And I knew that if the worst came to the worst I could always go back home. There would always be a bed and an open door for me in Barry.

I thought Loughborough would be a nice place to train, to get away from it all and be around a lot of different people. It would also mean that I was working with a young coach in Kevin Renshaw, with whom I'd had a good relationship in the past. I was instantly attracted to him in terms of what he had to offer me.

I settled in straight away at Loughborough. I enjoyed the group atmosphere, being around others who swam at the pool. British team-mates like Ross Davenport, David Carry, Liam Tancock, Caitlin McClatchey and British coaches such as Ben Titley and Ian Turner were there, so there was a lot going on.

Everything was on site. Physiotherapists were there for you, there is top sports science at the university, and it felt like a much more professional environment. You feel you're doing everything right, everything is catered for.

It was quite a contrast after spending thirteen years at Cardiff where, for me, everything had become stale.

Chapter Thirteen

2008 – an amazing year

So there I was, preparing for, and looking forward to, Olympic year and my foot problem flared up again.

This time, because I knew what had happened before, I was able to catch it very early. I was at home for the weekend that Wales won the Rugby Union Grand Slam and got checked out by the hospital. They confirmed that I had the same problem again but this time managed to get rid of it with intravenous drugs.

This happened the week before I was due to go to Eindhoven for the European Swimming Championships. Remember I'd never been to a 'long course', i.e. fifty-metre pool, version of the European Championships. I thought, oh brilliant, I'm not going to get to go again.

Then the doctor told me I could race, but that it had to be my decision. The foot was cleared up now and fit for swimming but it was only two days before I was due to go to Holland. Ultimately it was my decision and I said, "I'm going!" I'd done so many good training sets and it was the only major event I would be able to swim at before the Olympic Games.

It was weird getting back into the pool at Eindhoven as my foot was still a bit swollen and heavy and I'd lost some feeling in it. I was also taking medication in tablet form and it was quite strong, affecting my system and making my heart rate higher – it didn't feel natural.

The heats of the 1500 metres freestyle were really, really slow. I won the first heat and thought that I'd done enough, but when I looked at the time it was fifteen minutes eighteen seconds. I thought, I'm not going to be in the final, what have I done? I'd thought that I was coasting when actually I was dawdling.

I watched the next heats come in and luckily they were going slowly as well and I actually qualified second for the final. That was a real let-off because, if I'd been at the World Championships, it would have been the end. I would have been out straight away.

The final was a gutsy swim. I went for it quite fast and it did hurt towards the end, but I gritted my teeth and managed to come second, not too far behind Yuri Prilukov, in a time of fourteen minutes fifty-four seconds.

Given the circumstances that was pretty good, although if I'd been fully fit I think I could have gone quicker.

So it was a silver medal this time whereas, apart from the Commonwealth Games, I'd had bronze every time. It was a step up on the podium and I took a lot of positives out of it. I'd beaten the world champion Mateusz Sawrymowicz into third place. That was a massive thing for me. Now I just had to keep healthy.

At the Olympic trials, selection policy dictated that I couldn't swim my event for Beijing, as I was already qualified, so I did the 400 metres freestyle, which was something different and gave me some more confidence.

Then from the Olympic trials in Sheffield it was off to the World Short Course Championships taking place the following week at the Manchester Evening News Arena, which I didn't really want to do. But Britain was hosting the event, at another fantastic venue, so we had to do it.

I was training through it and feeling pretty rough but swam on the last day and won silver again. The order was the same as it had been in Eindhoven a few weeks earlier. Now I was out of the habit of getting bronze medals, with two silver medals inside a month and once again I'd beaten the world champion.

The crowd reaction was brilliant. Steve Parry, my team-mate from the Olympics in Athens, was doing the interviews poolside and he got them behind me. It was a full house on the Sunday afternoon and it was really nice to walk around, feeling that adulation. My family had driven up from south Wales, my sponsors were there too and I had the support of other swimmers who had got tickets for the day. And it was on prime time television on BBC2, which gave great exposure to the sport.

2008 was turning out to be the busiest year I'd ever had, with two major events in March and April, and the Olympics still to come, but that wasn't all. In May it was the World Open Water Championships in Seville, Spain.

I'd started doing the 10k event in South Africa in January, had enjoyed it, won the race and decided to go to Seville. I had to finish in the top ten to qualify for Beijing, and if I didn't do it I would knock it on the head. That would be the end of my Open Water adventure.

I kept to my plan, swimming from the front again, broke the pack, and the front of the field was reduced to three and then two. I had a huge tussle with Vladimir Dyatchin of Russia, who was to be disqualified in the Olympic final, going into the home straight around the last turning buoy. We were virtually swimming on top of each other, arms flying everywhere. He struck me on the chin once and I swallowed water and was sick. The water was dirty, but it was a calm, flat, straight river which was pretty much ideal for my first main Open Water event.

The photographs of the finish are amazing. I'm reaching for the pad after an hour and fifty-three minutes swimming and there is only a third of a second between us.

I'd come second again, which seemed to be the theme of the year, but I had qualified for the Olympics. It didn't seem like a World Championships, even though it was. The silver medal was great of course, but it was all about the qualification for Beijing.

Chapter Fourteen

Looking forward

The British public had really enjoyed the Beijing Olympic Games.

Rebecca Adlington, with her two gold medals in the 400 and 800 metres freestyle, had given us and the public the belief that a British swimmer could go out and beat the best in the world. In the past, British swimming had gone without medals at several major championships and the belief just hadn't been there.

Now others can be inspired by what Becky has done in the pool and what Keri-Anne Payne, Cassie Patten and I have achieved in the Open Water. The public have really taken to swimming and the sport has a new-found respect. Nowhere was that more obvious than when many of the Olympians and Paralympians were paraded in open-top buses in London on a cold day in mid October. I didn't know where to look because there were so many people around and we had to wave to them all. The number of people who turned out to greet us on a working day was incredible.

It felt like we'd won the FA Cup. It was similar to those pictures you see after a team has won at Wembley, or when England won the Ashes, only this time you're starring in it. It's almost too much: people hanging out of office windows, on the street, standing on top of parked cars and shouting your name. It takes a while to sink in but it's really enjoyable and makes you feel so proud. I got a few pictures on my camera phone of the masses of people in Trafalgar Square – all packed in like people on football terraces.

I was lucky enough to have an open-top bus parade in Cardiff as well. I saw a lot of people I knew, it was patriotic and very, very Welsh-themed. It was a Monday, a school day, and I was expecting the odd grandma or granddad to turn up, but lots of people made the effort and that's when you realise the effect that the team has had.

Once the big ordeal of a major Games is over, it's hard to imagine getting back into a pool again! That's why I took a long break after the Olympics – not only to recharge the batteries, but to enjoy myself and to get the hunger back.

But then you start missing training. I have to confess I felt terrible when I got back into the pool. I was a little overweight and I'd lost the feel for swimming. My body had, in effect, shut down for two months, at least where swimming was concerned.

Getting back into shape compares with the pre-season training that footballers do. It involves a lot of outdoor running, gym work, cycling, rowing and some hard slogs in the pool to build up the base for the aerobic work.

I'm now starting to get asked whether I will concentrate on pool swimming or competing in the Open Water competitions. But there is actually no such thing as an Open Water swimmer or a pool swimmer. I train full-time in the pool; all of my sets are geared towards racing better in the 1500 metres freestyle. That training is good enough to do Open Water as well. However, I will do more events to get more experience.

Everything is planned in great detail. At the Olympics in Beijing, we shipped over an ice bath for muscle-damage recovery; no one had ever done the event before so every angle had to be covered. I worked with a top cycling and marathon nutritionist to help deal with my carbohydrates and my recovery system.

2010 will be decision time in my life as to how the 1500 metres is going. That will be a target for the Commonwealth Games in Delhi. It'll be less than two years out from the London Olympics, and I'll be able to see how well I'm performing, in order to decide if I can compete at the top level.

Maybe I would be better off just doing the Open Water, but there's a lot of potential in both events and I have a strong desire to do both in London in 2012.

It's hard to believe that the London Olympics are less than four years away. The timing has fitted in so nicely with my career. When London was awarded the Games I was pleased but didn't realise how very big it would be. Now I can see just how massive it will be for athletes like me, to be competing there. Also it's so important for Britain to put on a great show. Hosting the Olympics now is so competitive.

However, I don't feel there's any extra pressure on the athletes to perform at a home Games. The governing bodies of the various sports may feel it, but, if anything, it should be easier for us because of the fantastic support we'll receive and the familiar surroundings. In football the crowd is sometimes called the twelfth man, so it should be like that for us.

I have always dreamed of retiring after my best performance or at a really big competition, where the memories will be amazing, at the very pinnacle of the sport. That's the best time to walk away and, hopefully, London 2012 will provide me with the best of both worlds and I will be able to hang my goggles up, happy, and have no regrets.

That's the plan as far as swimming is concerned, but of course there's more to life than swimming. I will miss it for certain, and it might take a while to get over the sadness of leaving so much behind, but I see myself going back to Cardiff, and living a normal life.

I hope that, whatever walk of life I do go into, I will have had enough experience to help me be strong in that environment. I'm only twenty-three now so I'm not thinking about having a family but when Davies junior eventually appears, if it's a boy, I might get him involved in football, rugby or golf.

I wouldn't be surprised if he was very sports-oriented!

I've become interested in working in the

Police Force or possibly as a teacher. Or maybe I will go into the media. I'm keeping my options open.

Whatever I end up doing, I want to be able to look at myself in the mirror and say that I gave my first career everything. And I'll have lots of brilliant memories and a stack of medals to show for it.

Inside Out

Real life stories from behind bars

Brought together by their crimes, the prisoners at Parc Prison, Bridgend, share their stories of life on the other side of the security walls.

Whether they are tough criminals or teenagers in trouble for the first time, they all have one thing in common – they had a life outside.

The prisoners have put into words what it's really like doing time at Parc Prison, how they got there and their hopes for the future.

These stories of their lives before crime will surprise and move you, make you laugh and cry in equal measures!

Royalties from this book will go to Parc Prison's arts and educational fund to support creative workshops for prisoners.

www.accentpress.co.uk

Black-Eyed Devils

Catrin Collier

One look was enough. Amy Watkins and Tom Kelly were in love. But that one look condemned them both.

'Look at Amy again and you'll return to Ireland in a box.' Amy's father is out to kill Tom.

All Tom wants is Amy and a wage that will keep them. But Tonypandy in 1911 is a dangerous place for Irish workers like Tom, who have been brought in to replace the striking miners. The miners drag them from their beds and hang them from lamp posts as a warning to those who would take their jobs.

Frightened for Amy, Tom fights to deny his heart, while Amy dreams of a future with the man she loves. But in a world of hatred, anger and violence, her dream seems impossible until a man they believed to be their enemy offers to help. But, can they trust him with their lives?

www.accentpress.co.uk

Alive and Kicking

Andy Legg

Andy Legg is one of the best-loved players in Welsh international football and his legendary long throw-in earned him a place in the record book.

One of a select few to play for South Wales arch-rivals Swansea City and Cardiff City, Andy played six times for Wales and more than 600 League games for Swansea, Notts County, Birmingham City, Peterborough, Reading and Cardiff.

But in 2005 his life was turned upside down when a lump in his neck turned out to be cancer. Alive and Kicking is Andy's emotional account of his treatment, his fears for his life and how the messages of support from his fans gave him the strength to fight on and return to the game.

www.accentpress.co.uk

Bring it Back Home

Niall Griffiths

Chased by a hit-man, a young man returns home from London to a small town in Wales. Reconciliation with his family is alternated with his pursuer's progress. A long criminal connection is revealed but can he escape the sins of his fathers?

This is a tense, tightly written drama that will captivate the reader with fast, gut-wrenching action.

www.accentpress.co.uk

The Rubber Woman

Lindsay Ashford

The world of Cardiff's sex trade hits the headlines when a woman is butchered and left for dead. Pauline distributes condoms to the women of the red light district and is known locally as 'the rubber woman'. She and Megan, a forensic psychologist, make it their mission to stop more women becoming victims. They don't know it yet, but one of them is already marked out for death.

www.accentpress.co.uk

Aim High

Dame Tanni Grey Thompson

Aim High reveals what has motivated Dame Tanni Grey Thompson, UK's leading wheelchair athlete, through the highs and lows of her outstanding career. Her triumphs, which include winning 16 medals, eleven of which are gold, countless European titles, six London Marathons and over 30 world records have catapulted this Welsh wheelchair athlete firmly into the public consciousness.

www.accentpress.co.uk

The Corpse's Tale

Katherine John

Dai Morgan has the body of a man and the mind of a child. He lived with his mother in the Mid Wales village of Llan, next door to bright, beautiful 19 year old Anna Harris. The vicar found Anna's naked, battered body in the churchyard one morning. The police discovered Anna's bloodstained earring in Dai's pocket.

The judge gave Dai life.

After ten years in gaol Dai appealed against his sentence and was freed. Sergeants Trevor Joseph and Peter Collins are sent to Llan to reopen the case. But the villagers refuse to believe Dai innocent. The Llan police do not make mistakes or allow murderers to walk free.

Do they?

www.accentpress.co.uk

The Hardest Test

Scott Quinnell

Scott Quinnell is one of the best-known names in rugby. He played both rugby league and rugby union, for Wales and for the British Lions. He was captain of the Welsh team seven times and won 52 caps.

But amidst all this success, Scott had a painful secret. He struggled to read. In *The Hardest Test*, he describes his struggle against learning difficulties throughout his childhood and his journey towards becoming one of the best rugby players in Britain. When he retired from rugby in 2005 he continued his battle with dyslexia in order to change both his and his children's lives.

www.accentpress.co.uk

Life's New Hurdles

Colin Jackson

Colin Jackson is one of the greatest athletes that Britain has ever produced. He was in the world top ten for 16 years, and was world number 1 for two of them. He set seven European and Commonwealth and nine UK records and he still holds the world record for indoor hurdling.

In 2003, Colin retired from athletics in front of an adoring home crowd. Then real life began. In *Life's New Hurdles* Colin describes the shock of adjusting to sudden change. From athletics commentating to sports presenting and *Strictly Come Dancing*, Colin describes the challenges and joys of starting a whole new life.

www.accentpress.co.uk

Vinyl Demand

Hayley Long

Beth Roberts and Rula Popek have a lot in common. They are both 19, both have crap jobs and both live in the worst flat in the whole of Wales.

The girls have no money, no boyfriends, family who are thousands of miles away and a final demand for a gas bill which they cannot pay. It all looks pretty bleak until one day when Rula stumbles across an entire vinyl record collection which has been left in a local charity shop. She takes a gamble and blows the money for the gas bill on the whole lot and the dream of becoming Cardiff's very own answer to the global girl DJ, Lisa Lashes. It's just a shame she didn't bother to explain the plan to Beth first.

www.accentpress.co.uk

Losing It

Roger Granelli

Losing It is set in the world of Baldock, local drug dealer and hard man of the Welsh Valleys. When one of his drug-runners, TJ, starts taking his own cut, it proves to be a big mistake. Baldock's reaction is explosive and violent.

Baldock's life is not straight forward. At home sits his dependent, wheelchair-bound father, a WWII veteran who has no idea about his son's drug empire. This taut father and son relationship is the backdrop to Baldock's increasingly desperate need to find and deal with TJ. Looking for TJ, Baldock neglects his father's needs with incendiary results that will change his life forever.

www.accentpress.co.uk

Quick Reads

Books in the Quick Reads Series

101 Ways to get your Child to Read	Patience Thomson
A Day to Remember	Fiona Phillips
Aim High	Tanni Grey Thompson
Alive and Kicking	Andy Legg
All These Lonely People	Gervase Phinn
Black-Eyed Devils	Catrin Collier
Bring It Back Home	Niall Griffiths
The Cave	Kate Mosse
A Cool Head	Ian Rankin
The Corpse's Tale	Katherine John
The Dare	John Boyne
Doctor Who: The Sontaran Games	Jacqueline Rayner
Dragons' Den: Your Road to Success	
The Hardest Test	Scott Quinnell
In At the Deep End	David Davies
Inside Out	Parc Prisoners
Life's New Hurdles	Colin Jackson
Losing It	Roger Granelli
Reaching for the Stars	Lola Jaye
The Rubber Woman	Lindsay Ashford
Secrets	Lynne Barrett-Lee
The Tannery	Sherrie Hewson
Vinyl Demand	Hayley Long

www.quickreads.org.uk.